A Pebble Dropped in Water

A Collection of Poetry for the Soul's Path to Enlightenment

Socrates The Messenger
Foreword by Angela Divine

The Awakened Press

The Awakened Press

www.theawakenedpress.com

For information about special discounts or for bulk purchases, please contact The Awakened Press at books@theawakenedpress.com.

The Awakened Press can bring authors to your live event.

For more information or to book an event contact books@theawakenedpress.com or visit our website at www.theawakenedpress.com.

Book and cover design by Kurt A. Dierking II

Printed in the United States of America

First The Awakened Press trade paperback edition

ISBN: 979-8-9870434-5-5

A Pebble Dropped in Water

A Collection of Poetry for the Soul's Path to Enlightenment

Socrates The Messenger

Foreword by Angela Divine

The Awakened Press

To my Father, who taught me how to Love, by Loving me unconditionally.

To Angela, my Earth Angel, who has stuck with me through the light and dark times.

To all my teachers and mentors, seen and unseen, who have helped me on my path of healing.

To the Source of my being, God, to which I give all the glory and credit, for it is from this source that these poems arise. I am the grateful and humble messenger.

Contents

Foreword   i

Introduction   v

The Messages

    A CHANNEL CRYSTAL CLEAR   1

    A LITTLE WAR WITHIN   3

    A NEW HUMAN RACE   5

    ALL THE GLORY GOES TO GOD   7

    ANGELIC HUMANS   9

    ASHES TO ASHES, DUST TO DUST   11

    BACK TO THE FOUNTAIN   17

    CLEAR DISCERNMENT   21

    CLOSER THAN THE BREATH   25

    DEEP WITHIN THE HEART   27

    DISTRACTIONS   29

    ENLIGHTENMENT   31

    FORGIVENESS IS THE ANSWER   35

    FREEDOM IS FREE   37

    FROM OUR HEAD DOWN TO OUR TOES   41

    GET GET GET   45

    GOD INSIDE US   49

    GRATITUDE   51

    HIDE AND SEEK   55

    HOLY SPIRIT FLOW   57

    I AM A HUMBLE MESSENGER   59

    I SAW GOD THE OTHER DAY   63

IN THE SILENCE, IN THE STILLNESS   67

INNER GLOW   71

LIFE IS REALLY SIMPLE   75

LIFE'S PURPOSE   79

LIKE A PEBBLE DROPPED IN WATER   81

LIVING IN THE QUESTIONS   85

LOVE FLOW THROUGH US   87

LOVE IS THE ANSWER   91

LOVE IS WHO WE ARE   93

LOVE IS   97

MEMORY   101

MIRACLES   103

MOTHER GAIA   105

NEVER DID I ROAM   107

NOWHERE TO SEEK   111

ONLY LOVE IS REAL   113

OUR PURPOSE IS TO LOVE   115

PATH OF LIGHT   117

PRACTICING PRESENCE   121

FREE AT LAST   125

SACRED STILLNESS   127

SINGULARITY   129

SOCRATES SPEAKS   131

SURRENDER THE FIGHT   133

SWEET AMAZING GRACE   135

THE BALANCED BREATH   137

THE BLAME GAME   139

THE BREATH OF LIFE   141

THE ELEMENTS   143

THE GIFT OF LIFE   147

THE GRACE OF GOD   149

THE LIGHT OF YOUR SOUL   151

THE MATRIX OF THE MIND   153

THE PATH OF LIGHT   157

THE SECRET TO CHANGE   159

THE SILENT WATCHER   163

THE SOUL'S RELIGION   167

THE SOUND THAT NATURE PLAYS   169

THE SWEETNESS OF SPIRIT   171

THE TAO   173

THE TREASURE WE SEEK   177

THE UNITY IN DUALITY   181

TIME   185

TO KNOW THYSELF IS THE ANSWER   189

TRANSFORMATION   193

TRUE LOVE IS AWAKENING   195

UNITY   197

WE ARE CO-CREATING   201

WE THE PEOPLE   203

WHAT IS LOVE   205

WHO WE ARE   209

HEARTS AND MINDS ALIGNED   213

About Socrates The Messenger   216

"See through the reality of duality"

I have been divinely appointed to write this foreword for my beloved Socrates, to shine more light on his work. A little about me. I love humanity and have a desire to serve those who are in need. I have been practicing as a holistic nurse and spiritual counselor for many years. My authentic, compassionate nature shines through when I am given the opportunity to assist others. I enjoy helping others go deep into mind, body, and spirit for clearer truth and healing. Socrates and I had many things in common that I will share below.

On my first date with Socrates, we went to a gathering with Chief Golden Eagle, where he acknowledged our connection. He said to me, "Go sit on his lap like you used to." He was referring to our past lives. Chief Golden Light Eagle asked us to stand next to him for two hours while he taught about the Universal and Spiritual laws of the Creator. Socrates felt that we got married that day. Many years later, at a large conference, Chief Golden Eagle called out, "Can the Angel and the Philosopher please stand up." We were astounded that he was acknowledging us again. We began to see that we had a profound reason to be together.

We are both passionate about sharing the trust

and love that we have learned to cultivate in our daily actions and attitudes. We served many together and even those without a place to live. We also enjoyed nature, gardening, and our cats. I had prayed for a partner to grow with me in life, and the Creator brought us together. Socrates was dedicated to deep spiritual growth through awareness of the light and dark within our relationship and individually.

One way to describe this is our alchemical relationship; being willing to sit in the fire of the ego to transform (burn away) the lower selves and integrate all healed aspects. Throughout our lives together, we encountered many different energies of duality, and we chose Love, freedom and inner knowing of Source. We were *willing* to sit in the fire of the alchemical process that moves through the dark and the light. His poetry does reflect this.

Right after finishing his book, he left our beautiful Earth and his kids who were cherished. Through many contacts with his spirit after leaving, he shared how joyful he is to be with Christ and learning how to serve even more from the spirit realm. Many of his friends also saw him in the spirit realm with Christ and Buddha in bliss. This has allowed me to be in a place of acceptance and peace. From the spirit realm right after he passed, he asked me to please share all that we have learned with many people, and this includes his poetry as a big part of that.

Socrates' dedication to knowing God and Christ

got stronger each year, and in 2013, out of the blue from the still-small voice inside, his first poem birthed forth. Each word flowed through his heart and is the foundation of his poetry. He said the first one was inspired from our friend Charles from Sedona, who lived his life like a saint. As Charles awakened each morning he said, "God put in front of me today the people we may serve." Charles had so many miracle stories from serving others through the Creator.

I was blessed to witness the birthing of each new poem and the Psalms that poured through him. Upon reflection, I found that Socrates was a Psalmist. A Psalmist moves in the prophetic music realm and is a gifted person. With sensitivity, discernment and creative talent, they receive and relay revelations from God to the listener. They are not practicing or training to be a Psalmist, they are selected by the Creator. They have been chosen and given anointing to be used as a unique prophetic "channel" for God to flow through. They will write their messages down in a secret place in meditation. Psalmists, like Socrates, desire to share with those who are sensitive to listen and connect with the mind and presence of God.

Socrates' desires in life were not centered on outside worldly things. He was interested in his connection with Source and friends and family. He loved meeting new open-minded people to share stories and poetry with. His poetry showed his journey seeing the contrast (yin and yang) in life, and then eventually, the realization of the perfection in all of it.

We used to say to each other, "The only thing is Love." As a healer and poet, his message and desire for humanity was to forgive yourself and others to your highest ability and willingness using allowance, surrender, and trust. Lastly, he wanted people to ask to be shown the hidden parts of themselves. He had a servant heart and wanted to help awaken himself and others to the truth he discovered. Socrates said one day, "My desire is to inspire you to seek and knock and find through the doorway of the heart beneath the busy mind. To look with eyes of innocence with forgiveness, then we're free. Free of judgment, conflict, suffering and pain. All fears stem from the belief in loss or gain. The belief in separation is the cause of all disease. For fear has many forms and varying degrees."

I am grateful for the opportunity to support him while he completed his Earthly mission in this life. I hope you are inspired by these poems (his legacy). May it touch your heart, enliven your soul, and awaken and open your mind to love more.

Many blessings to all.
Love,
Angela Divine

When you read Socrates' poems, go into your heart and read slowly to absorb the depth and richness of his messages.

"I know that I know nothing"

You hold in your hands words of wisdom, "channeled" in the form of poetry, from that one in history known as Socrates the Philosopher.

Socrates is most often considered to be the wisest of his time, because he said, "I know, that I know nothing."

He was reported to have never written anything down, so the words contained herein are a true treasure.

Ironically, in this life, my name is Socrates, and through an inner voice I was inspired to write what I am hearing. I have never sat down with the intention to write.

It usually happens during times of quiet meditation, in which I hear the first verse, reach for a pen and a pad, and the rest flows through in a few minutes.

Please do not hurry through each verse. Rather, allow each sentence to be heard within the heart, and each concept to fill the mind and the body, with its unique frequency or vibration.

May you be transformed, as your consciousness is raised, through allowing these ideas to inspire you to think differently.

A CHANNEL CRYSTAL CLEAR

I am the breath of life
I am Spirit, prana, chi
I am the resurrection
I am Soul, I am free

On the Earth I reside
In body, flesh, and bone
Of myself, I do nothing
But with God, I do atone

Transcending all the suffering
Forgiving all the pain
Ascending within consciousness
True Oneness, I attain

No more separation
No more doubt or fear
Completely liberated
My mind is crystal clear

Seeing only Love
The only thing that's real
Guided by the heart
Compassion I do feel

To live a life of service
Is my true desire
This, the highest purpose
To which I do aspire

This is the nature of the soul
The reason that I'm here
To be the Light and Love I Am
A channel crystal clear

An instrument of peace
A flame to light the way
That all beings may awaken
In the name of God, I pray.

A LITTLE WAR WITHIN

There is a little war within,
The psyche of right and wrong,
A duality, and polarity,
That don't seem to get along.

The separation is an illusion,
A trick of the right and left brain,
The identification with the ego self,
A reality, quite insane.

Yet, within the realm of the two,
That arose from the realm of the one,
The yin and yang of life,
The day, the night, of the sun.

The two, give birth to a third,
A Trinity divine,
The father, mother, and child,
A miraculous design.

For in the eyes of a babe,
The soul within, doth shine,
Before it's taught, right and wrong,
Theirs, and yours, and mine.

Then the little war begins,
Attached to things and stuff,
Taught reward and punishment,
Don't cry, just be tough!

Until we open, unto the heart,
Forgive the pain, suppressed,
The little war within will grow,
We'll never find true rest.

R.I.P. can be for the now,
Don't wait until you die,
End the little war within,
Open your heart and fly.

Freedom is our birthright,
It's not from blood and war,
Peace and love and harmony,
Is what this life is for.

A NEW HUMAN RACE

For those who will listen,
Who have ears to hear,
The thunder of silence,
Is crystal clear.

Beneath the noise,
Of the world you see,
Voices of ancestors,
From eternity.

Many secrets, much wisdom,
Is here in this place,
This time of awakening,
The human race.

It's time to slow down,
Step back, look around,
As what we call "progress,"
Just might take us down.

Life is so simple,
Just live and let live,
It's not what we get,
But what we can give.

The gifts that are given,
Are given to share,
No need for poverty,
No burdens to bear.

Supporting each other,
Is all that we need,
To solve all the problems,
Created by greed.

Remembering our Oneness,
Our essence the same.
Remembering our freedom,
It's time to reclaim.

Our sovereignty, our planet,
From those that control,
The illusion, the matrix,
Can't touch our soul.

Peaceful warriors of the rainbow,
Stand up, take your place,
In the power of Love,
For a new human race.

ALL THE GLORY GOES TO GOD

All the glory goes to God,
For this precious life I live,
I first receive, from this Source,
In everything I give.

Not from me, rather through me,
The fruits of Spirit flow,
When I ask, it's given me,
This truth, I've come to know.

I have no need, I have no lack,
To share is my desire,
Serving the atonement,
Baptized by Christ fire.

By the power, and the presence,
Of the Spirit, I abide,
In complete surrender
My heart, open wide.

Guided by true Love,
I have mastered fear,
The ego's voice is gone,
The truth is all I hear.

The wisdom from within,
In silence, it is heard,
From before time began,
In the beginning was the word.

In the beginning was the word,
And the word was a sound,
The vibration of Creation,
Emanating all around.

The mystery of life,
Manifests before my eyes.
The unseen, within form,
From nothing does it rise.

Humbling in its Majesty,
Yet, only just a dream,
Changing and transforming,
Like water into steam.

How it happens, no one knows,
It makes me stand in awe,
All the glory goes to God,
On Earth, this blue green ball.

ANGELIC HUMANS

I grew wings the other day,
As my heart burst out my chest.
I was freed of guilt and shame,
And all my past was blessed.

I almost died, as I transformed,
Floating in a state of bliss.
My essence as, one with God,
This truth, I can't dismiss.

I am you, and you are me,
The secret of our souls.
ALL is God, and ALL is Love,
It's written in the scrolls.

I have no doubt, and beyond faith,
For in my heart I know.
Who I Am, before the questions,
Before above, and, below.

Yet, on this Earth, I reside,
At this time and space.
Part of a grand awakening,
Transforming the human race.

We are human Angels,
It's time to claim our wings.
Free ourselves from limitations,
Beliefs in lesser things.

The power of Love is ours to wield,
The sword of truth reveals.
The end of an era, beginning anew,
Angels of the seventh seal.

The revelation, told by John,
Is happening as I speak.
A new Earth is rising,
Held by the humble and meek.

We shall inherit this new Earth,
As it says in Matthew, 5:5.
As angelic humans, guardians of life,
ALL beings will truly thrive.

ASHES TO ASHES, DUST TO DUST

Ashes to ashes,
Dust to dust,
The old world is crumbling,
It has to, it must.

Old systems, old programs,
Old patterns, old ways.
There is no such thing,
As "the good old days"

The government, politics,
Corporations, their crime,
The ones with the power,
Have had their time,

A new Earth is rising,
The Spirit reborn.
Grounded in truth,
Through the coming storm.

"Hold onto your hat,"
Be in your "right mind,"
Believe nothing you hear,
In the "news" that you find.

There is nothing "new,"
In the world that's outside,
It's one step behind,
It's seeking to hide.

"Knock, it'll be opened,"
"Seek, you shall find."
"Ask, and it is given,"
Be not, "left behind."

A smidgen of willingness,
Is all that you need,
Surrender, to Source,
Allow Spirit to lead.

We can't solve our problems,
With the thinking we used,
When they were created
We were confused.

We've been "bamboozled,"
By the powers that be,
We gave our allegiance,
To a flag that is not free.

Our freedom's inherent,
It cannot be bought.
"The American dream,"
The wars that we've fought.

It's ALL an illusion,
"The carrot" held high,
Chasing false happiness,
And Love, we can't buy.

We will never attain it,
Always one step behind,
It's never outside us,
Look inside, to find.

If you don't go within,
You will go without,
Lost in the darkness,
Full of fear and doubt.

"My yoke is easy,"
"My burden is light,"
Words spoken by a Master,
That's, "seen the Light."

There is nothing to fear,
There is no loss or gain,
No death as you know it,
No "thing" to attain.

Nothing, can add to,
Nor, take away,
From the Light of your Soul,
Awaken, I pray.

"It's" actually YOU,
Beyond name and form,
"It's" not something you have,
"It's" not something that's born.

The ultimate truth,
You're pure Spirit, pure Light,
The war is within,
Give up the fight.

For peace won't be found,
Or forced from outside,
But, remembered within,
In peace, we abide.

"Ashes to ashes,"
"Dust to dust,"
For the old world to crumble,
We choose it, we must!

BACK TO THE FOUNTAIN

I am a fountain,
Living water clear,
That all who thirst,
May draw near.

One with Source,
An endless flow,
Those seeking truth,
Thyself, to know.

The greatest wisdom,
Is found inside,
In sacred silence,
We can confide.

Deep in the stillness,
There is a voice,
Whether we listen,
Is our free choice.

The highest guidance,
From our God,
It gives us comfort,
Thy staff and rod.

When we surrender,
Our deepest prayer.
We will receive,
Then we can share.

Like a river,
To the sea,
One with Source,
Flowing free.

Giving life,
As it flows,
Along its banks,
Nature grows.

Without thought,
It simply gives,
Of itself freely,
Abundance lives.

Through its nature,
One with Source,
Wherever it goes,
It's right on course.

They say "All roads,
Lead to Rome,"
Back to the center,
Back to our Home.

Back to the fountain,
The endless flow,
No more seeking,
Thyself we know.

CLEAR DISCERNMENT

When one has clear discernment,
Beyond judgment, insecurities, and fear,
An open-hearted awareness,
Of the truth, the masters hold dear.

"I am Love," is the ultimate answer,
To all questions that arise,
For in the presence of the "I Am" self,
All illusions drop their disguise.

One sees the world, unbroken,
Regardless of the chaos at hand,
Temporarily under construction,
Following the "divine plan."

When we come into alignment,
In body, mind, and soul,
Listening to the silence,
Inner peace, as the goal.

We will release all of the tension,
The fear, the anger, and pain,
Healing the past transgressions,
Letting joy, and freedom reign.

This is the way to change things,
Not complaining, and getting upset,
Resistance, causes persistence,
More of the same, is what we'll get.

To believe it, before you see it,
The master magician's way,
Alchemy, and transformation,
The dawning of a brighter day.

A world where all are cared for,
The staving, the suffering, the poor,
The Earth, our Mother, is honored,
Awareness of what life is for.

For-giving, and sharing, and caring,
Our gifts, with love and joy,
Storing our treasures in Heaven,
Where moth and rust cannot destroy.

As we look at the current conditions,
We must see with our inner "third eye,"
It's all unfolding perfectly,
Don't watch the media's lies.

Continue to choose to love,
Forgive and let go of the past,
Follow the dream in your heart,
It is done unto you, as you ask.

When one has clear discernment,
Who's mastered the monkey mind,
In the moment, the secret of being,
The seeker of truth will find.

CLOSER THAN THE BREATH

Breathing in
Breathing out,
Inhaling faith,
Exhaling doubt,

Closer than the breath,
In the stillness of the mind,
Everything you're looking for,
Outside yourself, you'll find,

In the center of the heart,
Is the center of the soul,
The secrets of the Universe,
Revealed on sacred scrolls.

Of who you are, and why you're here,
And what you chose to be.
In this life, and lives of past,
And ones not yet to see.

In this moment, all are one,
With every breath you take.
So be in joy, and share your love,
The future, you will make.

A world of peace, and harmony,
A world where there's enough.
For everyone to thrive in life,
Not needing all the "stuff."

As we remember who we are,
Our future is at stake.
Shining light in darkness,
Helping others to awake.

To the unity and Oneness,
Of all the life on Earth.
The beauty of diversity,
All is of equal worth.

We truly are the ones,
That we've been waiting for,
To heal the lie of separation,
To open up the door.

To a new way of being,
Inspired by the soul.
Through our faith in action,
All is healed, all is whole.

DEEP WITHIN THE HEART

Focus on the flame that burns,
Deep within the heart,
The silent place, true Love's embrace,
Where God, we are a part.

Illumination, soft and pure,
A lamp that lights the way,
For inner guidance, inner wisdom,
For inner truth I pray.

The truth that's true always,
Our Source and we are One,
We are here to share our love,
Like sunbeams to the Sun.

Shining light in darkness,
Shadows disappear.
Awakening from the dream,
Dispelling all our fear.

A brand-new dawn, a brand-new day,
A brand-new world we see,
No more limitations,
Our hearts and souls are free.

No longer led by the mind,
Thoughts that hold us down,
Beyond thought, we will find,
Abundance all around.

As we sow, so shall we reap,
Universal law,
What is good, for the one,
Is good, for the all.

So, focus on the flame that burns,
Deep within the heart,
The Source of Light, the Source of Love,
Which we all are a part.

DISTRACTIONS

So much information,
Distractions in the news,
All the drama, all the hype,
Much judgment, many views,

What is good, what is bad?
Who can save the day?
A president, a government?
The taxes that we pay?

A system of division,
Built on fear and greed,
Injustices, corruption,
It's time to take the lead,

To take responsibility,
The ability to respond,
To realize, our true worth,
Not in a savings bond,

We are the ones to change things,
It's all happening inside,
The world is just reflecting,
That which we've tried to hide,

Honesty and courage,
Guided by the heart,
To see with eyes of innocence,
Forgiveness we impart,

When we look upon the world,
And smile at all we see,
Like a mirror, it will reflect,
The truth that sets us free,

All events are neutral,
It's how we choose to perceive,
That's creating all our future,
From whatever we believe,

So what is it in your consciousness?
What is your true desire?
To look upon the world with Love,
Is all it will require.

ENLIGHTENMENT

In unity consciousness,
There's no longer a fight.
No good guys or bad guys,
No darkness, or light.

The battles between them,
Duality's game.
The illusion of opposites,
Their essence the same.

Under the layers,
Of the human mind,
The patterns of polarities,
True peace you will find.

The presence of God,
A heart full of bliss,
Pervading all space,
Be not remiss.

In making an effort,
In taking the time,
To commune with the stillness,
The Oneness, divine.

All of your problems,
Suffering, and pain,
Will dissolve into nothing,
Truth will remain.

There's really no "you,"
As separate from "they,"
An identity, as personal,
The games that we play.

No winners or losers,
No better or worse,
No god, or devil,
No blessing, or curse.

One must be willing,
To let go of the "I,"
The illusion of specialness,
The ego must die.

If true enlightenment,
Is what you desire,
You must be ready,
To be baptized by fire.

Burning away,
Selfishness and pride,
Attachment to things,
The inequities inside.

Forgiveness of everything,
Unconditional Love,
Total acceptance,
Below, and above.

Freedom is here,
Heaven on Earth,
Within you and me,
Is where it will birth.

FORGIVENESS IS THE ANSWER

Every breath is a ceremony,
Every thought, a prayer.
Every emotion from the heart,
Affects the world we share.

Forgiveness is the answer,
To judgment, and the pain.
Unconditional Love for all,
The Oneness, which we came.

Gather together in circles of one,
Creating a sacred space.
Like a pebble dropped in water,
Touching the whole human race.

The seeds we plant are potent,
With nurture, water, and care.
Together we grow this garden,
With abundance, for all to share.

Listening to the feminine,
For wisdom, guidance, and grace.
Letting go of the masculine way,
That's destroying the human race.

Keeping our hearts wide open,
Humble, powerful, and pure.
Walking a path of beauty,
We the people, are the cure.

FREEDOM IS FREE

Freedom is free,
We choose to believe,
With violence and war,
It cannot be achieved.

Only remembering,
Our essence and soul,
Love is our weapon,
Peace is our goal.

Lay down your sword,
Raise the white flag,
Surrender to Source,
The cat's out of the bag.

War is a business,
Owned by the "elite,"
Their motive is money,
Their balance sheets.

They care not for life,
For mercy or grace,
Their goal is controlling,
The whole human race.

We must speak our truth,
Stand up and proclaim,
The unity and Oneness,
From where we all came.

The Earth is our Mother,
For us to take care,
Her abundance of resources,
For all life to share.

There is more than enough,
For all life to thrive.
To give, not to get,
Is why we're alive.

Our brothers and sisters,
Our neighbor as well,
For us to awaken,
The truth to tell.

One by one we emerge,
And stand in our might,
From darkness, and ignorance,
From blindness, to sight.

We are the Light,
The truth and the way,
Fighting for freedom is over,
It's time to play!

FROM OUR HEAD DOWN TO OUR TOES

We accept the Love of God,
From our head down to our toes,
Our cup, runneth over,
As a fountain flows.

A self-sustained polarity,
Connected, one with Source,
A channel, crystal clear,
For the greatest force,

This Source is Love, this Source is Light,
From this Source comes all we see,
Every soul, a part,
Of one big tapestry.

Weaving different colors,
Different forms, different shapes,
Its nature, transformation,
Like creating wine from grapes.

A bittersweet duality,
The realm of light and dark,
The seemingly separate universes,
Evolving from One spark.

Infinite dimensions,
Existing in one place,
All of it, here and now,
There is no time or space.

Yet, we are blessed, on this Earth,
A place to live and grow,
To remember, we are love,
And allow our Love to flow.

When we give, we receive,
Yet, there is no loss or gain,
Only transformation,
The seed, the plant, the grain.

All of life's a circle,
No beginning, and no end,
Death is an illusion,
It's fear we can transcend.

When we enter into the heart,
Relax, and become still,
We can feel and know the truth,
Our cup will start to fill.

A self-sustained fountain,
Springs forth and overflows,
We become the Love of God,
From our head down to our toes.

GET GET GET

Get, get, get,
How much can we get?
Programmed by the matrix,
We're trapped in its net.

Hypnotized, conformed,
By what's on the T.V. set,
Gimme, gimme, mine, mine,
I really need to get.

Get a job, get a car,
Get a perfect spouse,
Don't just get by, get more stuff,
Stuff it in a house.

When it gets old, get rid of it,
Go out and get some more,
The more you get, the better,
For"get" about the poor.

When do I get a raise?
When do I get paid?
Maybe I'll get lucky,
Maybe I'll get laid.

How can I get attention?
How many "likes" did I get?
Can I get some validation?
    I haven't gotten it yet.

    Perhaps if I get rich,
And purchase my own jet,
Maybe then I'll get respected,
While drowning in my debt.

The cycle of consumption,
    What else can we get?
All the while we're empty,
From the Love that we kept.

Have a seat, I will serve you,
    Your table I have set,
I'll give you food, I'll give you drinks,
    How much tip will I get?

Take a vacation, take a break,
Take a day, down by the lake,
Take a shower, take a nap,
Get some take-out, take a crap.

It's time to "get" back to the truth,
The answer's in the heart,
In our getting, and our taking,
Give a smile, just to start.

Life is not for-getting,
It's not the way to live,
Me, me, me, my, my, my,
It's better to for-give.

To live, is to give,
Without expecting back,
The more we give wholeheartedly,
We'll never live in lack.

GOD INSIDE US

So many are looking for God,
As an invisible, external thing,
The Creator of Heaven and Earth,
Not beggar, nor sinner, but King.

The One who's exalted on high,
Conceived of a virgin birth.
The truth is they have it quite wrong,
All life is of equal worth.

No better or worse, no Heaven or Hell,
Unless you believe in your mind.
The heart knows the truth, it sees with God's eyes,
We must look there, if we want to find.

The keys to the kingdom, the treasure of treasures,
Are here at our beck and call.
No need to suffer, to think ourselves less,
No matter how much we fall.

For when we are down, depressed and discouraged,
With nowhere to run or hide,
Is when we surrender, to that we call God,
And Love bursts our hearts open wide.

This is the magic, the miracle and healing,
That comes from our darkest of days.
For God is within us,
As us, beside us,
In everything, in everyone,
All-ways.

GRATITUDE

The purest prayer is gratitude,
Another day to live,
The simple things, the breath of life, to feel,
A heart to give.

Giving and receiving,
One and the same,
To live this law of life,
The reason that we came.

The ego wants to get,
A lower way to be,
The nature of the soul,
Gives of itself, and it's free.

It knows, it's One with Source,
No fear, or lack, or greed,
Its purpose is to share,
In everything we need.

Miracles are happening,
Every blink of an eye,
Every beat of the heart,
Without blood, we would die.

Eyes to see, ears to hear,
To speak, to taste, to touch,
A whole lot to be grateful for,
Why withhold so much?

There is enough for all to share,
The abundance of the Earth,
So much is wasted, so much trash,
It's time to see her worth.

Her spirit, and her body,
Spinning free in space,
No separate countries or borders,
One big human race.

A unified diversity,
Of unique and different tribes,
The mixing of the languages,
Resonating various vibes.

Seven colors of the rainbow,
Seven notes on the scale,
The seventh seal has broken,
The lifting of the veil.

To see the bigger picture,
That all of life is One,
We pray a prayer of gratitude,
For the rising of the sun.

HIDE AND SEEK

Hide and seek,
The game we play,
Looking for our self,
While running far away.

One of us is counting,
While the other of us hides,
Looking outside ourselves,
While in the heart, the Soul abides.

What a clever hiding spot,
The last place that we look,
The answer's always been here,
Not found in any book.

It's said, "the letter kills,"
Yet, "life, the Spirit brings,"
Storing treasures in Heaven,
Instead of stuff and things.

Seeking meaning and happiness,
In a world that's lost its way,
Is like looking for a needle,
In a giant stack of hay.

The path is straight and narrow,
The scales, they never lie,
When the heart is light as a feather,
In Spirit, we will fly.

We'll see the bigger picture,
The truth, from on high,
That which we've been looking for,
Is a love we cannot buy,

To have it, we must give it,
The Love of God is free,
We'll find, when we stop looking,
And hiding behind a tree.

It's time that we quit counting,
Remove our hands from our eyes,
Stop hiding from ourselves,
If we want to self-realize.

Then the game is over,
And a new one has begun,
For we have found ourselves,
Now it's time to have some fun.

HOLY SPIRIT FLOW

In me, as me, through me,
Holy Spirit flow,
I surrender to thy will,
Thy wisdom, may I know.

The highest truth that's always true.
That God and I are One.
No separation in between,
A sunbeam to the sun.

Extending Light unto the world,
The Light that never fails.
Extending Love unto all life,
For Love always prevails.

Such sweetness in its essence,
I want more, that I may give,
Empty of the "little self"
That God, through me may live.

This is the grand dichotomy.
That God and we are One.
We are the Light of the World,
As sunbeams to the Sun.

So stop waiting for a savior,
Someone to make you whole.
To solve the problems of the world,
The answer's in our Soul.

To know it, we must be it,
Beyond the facts we're told.
You must still the mind to feel it,
In the heart, you will behold.

In you, as you, through you,
The Holy Spirit flows.
When you choose to feel it,
Only God within you knows.

I AM A HUMBLE MESSENGER

I am a humble messenger,
This life is not my own,
I sit in silent prayer,
And share what I am shown.

These words are not from me,
Rather from an inner voice,
Listen if you will,
You always have free choice.

The world is an illusion,
Of mirrors and of smoke.
Nothing seen is solid,
This, the cosmic joke.

Your life is just a memory,
It fades away in time,
You'll never find success,
On the ladders that you climb.

All events are neutral,
There is no loss or gain,
You never are a victim,
In your suffering and pain.

Because you've been identified,
With separation and fear,
When the Soul awakens,
Awareness will be clear.

The "you" you think is "you,"
Is not the "you" that you thought,
You'll never find "the self,"
In all that you have sought.

When you let go of seeking,
And striving to attain,
Resting in remembrance,
True knowledge, you will gain.

In the world, not of it,
A sandbox to create,
Building castles in the sand,
Then crumbling to their fate.

For all you see of form,
Arises and passes away,
A temporary dimension,
To enjoy, laugh, and play.

Seriousness is of the ego,
In the shadows it is lost,
Trying to keep itself alive,
At any, and all cost.

When you become the witness,
Seated in the Soul,
Nothing will affect you,
You'll know that you are whole.

I am a humble messenger,
This life's not mine to claim,
My desire is to serve the Light,
Not specialness or fame.

I SAW GOD THE OTHER DAY

I saw God the other day,
It didn't have a face.
Everywhere, and nowhere,
Before time and space.

Everything, and nothing,
The I Am that I Am.
A single point of consciousness,
When all of life began.

I saw God the other day,
In the "good," and in the "bad,"
The biggest, and the smallest,
The happy, and the sad.

The secret of the Trinity,
The mystery of life.
The beauty, and the balance,
The harmony, of strife.

I saw Unconditional Love,
I saw the love, in the pain.
The wisdom, of equality,
In every loss and gain.

I saw polarities, dualities,
How opposites attract.
The movement in the spiral,
One expands, one pulls back.

Equal opposites in everything,
And Love has made it all.
No Heaven or Hell to praise or fear,
The reason for the "fall."

From the garden, Adam and Eve,
Tempted by the snake,
The fruit of the tree of knowledge, that,
"Good" and "evil" WE can make.

Created fear, guilt, and shame,
The chains that bind our soul.
Only WE can free ourselves,
And remember, we are whole.

To find our way back from this dream,
We must look inside our heart.
See the truth, that ALL is "God"
Every, single, part.

I saw God the other day,
Within all time and space.
I'm seeing God in EVERYTHING,
In every person's face.

IN THE SILENCE,
IN THE STILLNESS

Beyond words, beyond thoughts,
Beneath the movement of the mind.
In the silence, in the stillness,
Our Soul's essence, we will find.

Sweet surrender, pure awareness,
Floating in a sea of bliss,
Permeated, hypnotized,
Paralyzed by Soul's kiss.

This is Home, the zero point,
Once felt, one can't forget,
Until one tastes, one will hunger,
And always be in debt.

By its grace, one will live,
In pure gratitude and joy,
This is the treasure of Heaven,
Moth and rust cannot destroy.

This is our only purpose,
Our one true heart's desire,
Don't buy in to the lie,
That things and stuff we must acquire.

The world of form is temporary,
Distractions to the Soul,
Programs by the matrix,
Designed to control.

We're already free and sovereign,
Children of the Sun,
We are the Light of the World,
We are many, we are One.

Co-creating with our Source,
Anything we choose,
Where two or more are gathered,
In Love, we'll never lose.

All we need to do,
Is be silent, and be still,
The threshold of all wisdom,
The clear and perfect "will."

Not conformed by the world,
Or the programs in the mind,
But our consciousness transformed,
By the inner truth, we'll find.
Beyond words, beyond thoughts,

Our Soul's essence does reside,
In the silence, in the stillness,
Our heart's voice will be our guide.

INNER GLOW

In the stillness,
There's a gentle flow,
My cup runneth over,
From an inner glow.

A self-sustained,
Fountain of bliss,
A pervading ecstasy,
A Holy kiss.

So subtle and sweet,
Yet commanding and strong,
A feeling of Home,
Where I truly belong.

The essence of me,
Beyond physical form,
The womb of Love,
Where I'm reborn.

No doubt, or fears,
No guilt or shame,
Without limitations,
Suffering or pain.

A blissful awareness,
A source divine,
Radiating, permeating,
Universal mind.

A sense of dissolving,
Becoming one with the One,
An inner light shining,
As bright as the sun.

Our true identity,
Beyond our name,
Remembering ourselves,
Within duality's game.

Life is but a dream,
In the blink of an eye,
It will be over,
But we never die.

We are infinite choice,
Eternal and free,
Ever transforming,
Pure energy.

In the stillness,
You will know,
And feel your presence,
As an inner glow.

LIFE IS REALLY SIMPLE

Life is really simple,
Just be patient, and be kind,
Allow the grace of God,
To fill your heart, transform your mind.

Cherish every moment,
Don't waste your time in fear,
Being fully present,
"Rest in peace" while you're here.

There is no past or future,
The only time is now,
Life is really simple,
Like the teachings of the Tao.

Look to nature for wisdom,
The cycles of life and death,
Born into a body of flesh,
Into Spirit, at last breath.

Infinite, eternal,
The journey of the Soul,
No beginning and no end,
Like a circle, you are whole.

To live in joy and gratitude,
No matter what's around,
With an open heart to serve,
True happiness is found.

Life is really simple,
When we just believe,
That we are One with God,
All glory we'll receive.

How much will you allow?
What is your true desire?
Surrendering your intentions,
The Universe will conspire.

We'll know our higher purpose,
Aligned with true Love's will,
Hearing inner guidance,
The voice that's small and still.

Life is really simple,
Relax, and breathe, and smile,
Treat your neighbor as yourself,
You're only here a short while.

Sparks of divinity,
We're many, we are One,
Shining Light unto the world,
Like sunbeams to the Sun.

Transforming all the suffering,
Sickness, and dis-ease,
Awakening the human soul,
The ego, we appease.

Life is really simple,
Just let it be, let it be,
Accept the love and grace of God,
And extend it out for free.

LIFE'S PURPOSE

Just upon awakening,
Before I open my eyes,
I take a moment to ponder,
Some time to realize,

All that I am grateful for,
Another day to live,
The purpose of my life's become,
How can I love and give?

Seeing only beauty,
The essence of all things,
Regardless of appearances,
From fear, the ego clings.

Freedom is in letting go,
The prison of the mind,
Judging life as right or wrong,
Peace, we'll never find.

Within the wisdom of the heart,
Void of doubt and fear,
There is a voice that speaks the truth,
With vision crystal clear.

It is the Light of God,
The only thing that's real,
Shining forgiveness on the past,
In surrender, do we heal.

When we open up our eyes,
From the darkness, which we slept,
The dreamer of the dream awakens,
Into the Light we've stepped.

Where all is Holy and beautiful,
In how we choose to perceive,
We're in the realm of knowing,
Beyond what we believe.

The consciousness of miracles,
A shift in how we see,
Looking out, knowing all is Love,
This truth will set us free.

Just upon awakening,
Before you open your eyes,
Take a moment to ponder,
Some time to realize…

LIKE A PEBBLE DROPPED IN WATER

Like a pebble dropped in water,
As we drop into the heart,
Creates a ripple through the field,
Love's true essence, we impart.

Vibrates out, to the edge,
Of the Universe, and comes back,
As we give, we do receive,
And we'll never live in lack.

From this Source of living water,
Bubbling up like a spring.
For all to drink, and never thirst,
Things the world can never bring.

For the world is only temporary,
Things arise and pass away.
Yet, our Spirit and our Soul,
Keeps on growing, as we pray.

Praying not, for things unseen,
Nor for anything to be changed.
But praising God for all we have,
That we may not be deranged.

For life is always giving us,
Whatever we believe.
If we believe in fear and lack,
That's what we will receive.

So look within to find the roots,
The patterns in the mind.
Pull them up, till the soil,
The seed of truth you'll find.

You are worthy, you are loved,
You're forgiven, you are free.
You're pure Spirit, undefiled.
In your heart, you hold the key.

Release yourself from bondage,
Limitation, lack, and shame.
Look in the mirror, and love yourself,
Without judgment and or blame.

For you are loved and you are loving,
You are lovable forever!
If you could see through God's eyes,
You wouldn't doubt it, never.

So like a pebble dropped in water,
Drop into your heart.
Feel the truth of who you are,
And Love you will impart.

LIVING IN THE QUESTIONS

What, where, who?
When, how, why?
Living in the questions,
Is living to just get by.

Uncertainty and chaos,
In the outside world we see,
Searching for the truth,
The one that set us free.

I can only guide you,
Point you to the way,
To infinite wisdom, perfect peace,
Now, not "some day."

Beneath the roar and din of the world,
Closer than the breath,
Is the consciousness of Oneness,
Transcending life or death.

Where every cell dissolves,
Into Universal Mind,
An ecstatic blissful state,
The true self, you will find.

It's Love that you will feel,
Like you've never felt before,
It will take your breath away,
And leave you wanting more.

For you will have tasted,
The only thing that's real,
Not the love in your fairy tales,
Rather, one that you can feel.

Not from an outside source,
A person, place, or thing,
It's been with you always,
Right underneath your wing.

In the heart it rests,
Seek no more, and you will find,
Then, you'll live in your truth,
Not the questions in your mind.

One is an illusion,
The other one is real,
You'll know which one you're living,
By the way that you feel.

LOVE FLOW THROUGH US

Love, Love flow through us,
Through the thoughts in our mind,
Fill our hearts to overflowing,
Through our eyes, where we are blind.

Use our hands, to touch with,
Our voice, to speak what's true,
Our ears to hear, only Love,
Our bodies, make anew.

Transform within our consciousness,
All that's based in fear,
The belief in separation,
That the ego holds so dear.

We surrender to the higher will,
A life lived in the flow,
Living life with kindness,
Compassion, we bestow.

Goodness and mercy shall follow us,
On the straight and narrow way,
The way that takes no effort,
But to believe, and pray.

Making ourselves available,
With open hearts to give,
This is the highest purpose,
The gracious way to live.

But, first we must receive
The Light from which we've come,
Believe that we are worthy,
Remember where we're from.

We shine forth from Source,
As sunbeams to the Sun,
We are the Light of the World,
We are many, we are One.

The Earth, our precious Mother,
She's ours to treat with care,
She's been so disrespected,
It's become too much to bear.

Her elements, out of balance,
Disharmony, disease.
A reflection of our inner states,
I'm begging, could we please.

Take some time to ponder,
Allowing love to flow,
Healing our transgressions,
That we may come to know.

That Love is the answer,
The only thing that's real,
Allow it to move through us,
That we and Earth may heal.

LOVE IS THE ANSWER

Are you still living the questions?
Looking, for a clue?
What's the purpose and meaning of life?
Why are you here? What is true?

Who, and what you are?
The question that pierces the veil.
The answer is not so far,
How long will you keep chasing your tail?

Circles within circles,
Spiraling up and down,
In the center of your vortex,
The all-seeing eye is found.

The Seat of the Soul is waiting,
For you to sit, and quiet the mind,
Enter the altar of stillness,
Tap into your heart and find,

The Source of life that you're living,
Self-sustained, eternal, and free,
Infinite in its expression,
In the realm of duality.

The answer to all the questions,
One must find, in their own being,
To give you a hint, a clue,
It's not what the eyes are seeing.

The beauty of all the differences,
The diversity of the ONE,
The colors of the rainbow,
Mother Earth, Father Sun.

All a part of Creation,
The consciousness of the NOW,
Where everything is connected,
The mystery of the Tao.

The question that cannot be answered,
The answer can only be lived,
To LOVE, EVERYTHING, UNCONDITIONALLY,
Everything, we must forgive.

LOVE IS WHO WE ARE

Holy Mother, Holy Father,
I am thy Holy Child,
I am the life, the truth, the way,
Pure Spirit, undefiled.

Beyond time, beyond space,
Yet, on this planet I reside,
My purpose, to remember,
The Kingdom of Heaven's inside.

All the power, all the glory,
All the treasures that we seek,
Are ours to hold with care, to share,
When we're humble, pure, and meek.

Here and now is all there is,
Surrender, and let go,
Past and future fade away,
The weight we used to tow.

Open our hearts, spread our wings,
See how high, we can fly,
Letting go of doubt and fear,
The lie that we can die.

Eternal, and immortal,
Beings of Light and Love,
Heaven on Earth is ours to be,
So below, as above.

Forgiveness is the doorway,
Look within to find the key,
With a childlike curiosity,
Innocent and free.

Any darkness that you see there,
Is held within the Light,
When seen again with eyes of Love,
Blindness becomes sight.

I was lost, but now I'm found,
The grace of God prevails,
I am free of suffering,
The cross and the nails.

Resurrected from within,
I've been here all along,
No more separation,
No more right or wrong.

All there is, is Love,
And Love will find the way,
Love is who we are,
No matter what they say.

LOVE IS

It's said love is patient,
It's said love is kind,
Within the world now,
It's not easy to find.

Love God with the heart,
The mind, and the soul.
Your neighbor as yourself,
"The golden rule."

What can we do,
To enter the gate?
Become like a child,
No judgment, no hate.

A heart that is pure,
Innocent and free,
Is the doorway to Heaven,
To which Love is the key.

"By their fruits, you shall know them,"
A great master once said.
All talk and no action,
Is faith that is dead.

These are the leaders,
We've given our trust.
Their motive is money,
Power, and lust.

For things that don't serve us,
Or our beautiful Earth,
It's time to wake up,
It's time to give birth.

To a new way of being,
Led by the heart,
Remembering our essence,
Is where we must start.

Spiritual beings of Light,
Eternal and free.
Our thoughts are creating,
The world which we see.

It's time to stand up,
Together we claim,
The unity and Oneness,
From where we all came.

Transforming the world,
From the inside out,
Our vision of peace.
Never we doubt.

Our faith is in Love,
With the action we take,
Serving, and giving,
For goodness sake.

MEMORY

Memory, remember,
Remembering what is true,
Beyond thoughts, in the mind,
A feeling, through and through.

A rainbow of emotions,
In a suit of flesh and bone,
A living breathing storehouse,
Where mysteries are known.

Every cell an entity,
Intelligent by design,
All the different systems,
Together, intertwine.

A network of synapses,
Neurons that exchange,
Electrical chemical signals,
Allows life to rearrange.

Tapping into memories,
Deep in our hearts to feel,
Remembering all our parts,
Remembering what is real.

Bliss is the barometer,
The highest state to be,
Only when we're in it,
Can our love be true and free.

Bliss is our natural state,
Our thoughts have obscured,
When we let go of thinking,
It's present, rest assured.

It's really just that simple,
Quiet the mind and see,
You'll remember who you are,
A blissful memory.

MIRACLES

"As you believe, it is done unto you,"
True words a great master once said.
Faith is the key that opens the door,
  To miracles, and raising the dead.

"You shall do all these things, and greater things
  shall you do,"
He said, after healing the blind.
They watched in amazement, his power to heal,
  Not understood by the human mind.

The heart must be pure, thoughts still and clear,
  To see through the eyes of God.
No condition too big, as it may appear,
  The power of thy staff and thy rod.

Allows for the law of Oneness and Love,
  To overcome anything that we face.
As we navigate through the material world,
  Awakening the human race.

Do you remember the truth of your Soul?
  The Light which you are, and are from?
God in you, as you, and through you.
Heaven on Earth, thy kingdom come.

MOTHER GAIA

I am your Mother,
I give you my life,
The way that you treat me,
Cuts like a knife.

My body bleeds,
It weeps and shakes,
You poison my oceans,
Rivers and lakes.

You rape my body,
You poison the air,
When you chop the trees,
You're cutting my hair.

The oxygen you breathe,
Is life itself,
The animals you kill,
Trophies on a shelf.

Nothing seems sacred,
You've lost your way,
ALL life is precious,
WAKE UP, I pray.

Before it's too late,
And my nature can't give,
There'll be nothing left,
For your life to live.

From deep in my heart,
I'm holding the space,
With forgiveness, compassion,
Mercy and grace.

Patiently waiting,
For you to awaken,
My endless love,
Will not be forsaken.

For I have a plan,
And it involves you,
To remember your Mother,
And all that is true.

NEVER DID I ROAM

I forgive myself for judging,
Condemning, right or wrong,
Anyone or anything, myself,
My whole life long,

My "enemies," my "saviors,"
Pointing me back Home,
A place within my heart and soul,
Where never did I roam,

A resting place, a place of peace,
Beyond my name and form,
In the silence, in the stillness,
The eye of the storm,

From perception, "right" or "wrong,"
Comes the ego's voice,
If I listen to its lies,
I surrender my free choice,

To see the world as beautiful,
To see it through Love's eyes,
To reveal the truth of innocence,
To remove the false disguise,

To see the Light of God in all,
To truly self-realize,
To release the little self,
To all its hooks and ties,

In knowing deep within my core,
My Oneness with the Source,
My Oneness with everything,
"The way" I need not force,

It radiates outside me,
A flame that burns within,
Transmuting all the darkness,
That, which we call sin,

Are really misperceptions,
Clues along the path,
That guide me on the straight and narrow,
Transcending all my wrath,

God is Love, it does not punish,
Nor reward, for what I do,
Yet, from my thoughts, are effects,
Reflects my point of view,

If I don't like what I see,
It's time to look inside,
For what I see is what I get,
This truth, I cannot hide,

I can ignore, I can project,
Pretend it is not there,
It will not leave, it will not heal,
Until I kneel in prayer,

Surrender all I think I know,
My judgments, "good" and "bad,"
Openhearted, letting go,
Of things I thought were "sad,"

Knowing they were lessons,
Signposts pointing Home,
Remembering from where I came,
Where never did I roam.

NOWHERE TO SEEK

There is nowhere to seek,
Nor is there any place to go,
The spiritual journey, an inside job,
Within thyself to know.

When you remember who you are,
Beyond your name and form,
Before the many memories,
Before ego fear was born.

What's true is true always,
"The truth that sets you free,"
You are One with God,
And with everything you see.

No matter how many journeys,
In the illusion of what appears.
When you let go of seeking,
The journey's end is near.

A destination without distance,
To a goal that stays the same,
Resting in your heart and soul,
No judgment, guilt, or shame.

Everything is consciousness,
"Universal mind,"
Treat your neighbor as yourself,
Loving, patient, kind.

It's time for you to wake up,
From nightmares dreamt asleep,
Enlightened and awakened,
From a hypnotic trance so deep.

The belief in separation,
The root cause of all dis-ease,
Is only misperception,
Clouds passing in a breeze.

To "know thyself" is the answer,
Nowhere outside to seek,
The Kingdom of Heaven's within,
Known by the humble and meek.

ONLY LOVE IS REAL

From the place of inner stillness,
The path of Light's revealed,
With every beat of my heart,
I see the world as healed.

Nothing left to fix or save,
For I have seen the Light,
That pierces through duality,
The veil of "wrong or right."

Just beneath the surface,
You can feel it, if you try,
That "only Love is real,"
Is the truth, it's not a lie.

The experience of suffering,
Is from denying that this is true,
The belief in separation,
Or oneness, is up to you.

How we perceive, reveals in form,
In whatever we behold,
It's manifesting 'from' us,
Not 'to' us, as we're told.

We are the cause, not the effect,
Of the material world we see,
We can create it, anyway,
Our desire, our will is free.

Life then becomes a playground,
Building castles in the sand,
Enjoying every moment,
On this God-given promised land.

"The land of milk and honey,"
Of bounty, oh so sweet,
"Heaven," "the garden of Eden,"
Is right here, beneath our feet.

It seems that we've forgotten,
That "only Love is real,"
If only we re-member,
Then everything would heal.

OUR PURPOSE IS TO LOVE

May all minds awaken,
May all hearts feel,
The presence in the stillness,
Where peace and love are real.

No more questions, no more doubt,
No uncertainty, or fear,
We are One with our Creator,
The truth is crystal clear.

Just beneath the breath,
Pervades amazing grace,
Receive it in the silence,
The present, Holy place.

In complete surrender.
Allowing it to flow,
The living Light of Source,
Within, begins to grow.

Our cups runneth over,
With gratitude we share,
Every beat of our heart,
Every thought a prayer.

Extending the good and Holy,
OUR PURPOSE IS TO LOVE,
Creating Heaven on Earth,
So below, as above.

PATH OF LIGHT

Your personal point,
Of power and grace,
On the infinite path,
In time and space.

Is a presence felt,
Not to be named,
Beyond words and thoughts,
Cannot be claimed.

A blissful awareness,
A frequency divine.
Permeating everything,
Universal mind.

Infinite wisdom,
Perfect peace,
Ideas of self,
We must release.

The I Am, That I Am,
One with the One.
Heart light as a feather,
Soul bright as the sun.

Radiating outward,
From a bottomless well.
Filling all space,
Heaven to Hell.

What we call darkness,
Void of light.
Is the womb of Creation,
Where dualities unite.

Millions of galaxies,
In the darkness of space.
Embracing all life,
The human race.

As vast as it is outward,
It goes inward the same.
The Earth we call Gaia,
Is where we all came.

To learn how to love,
To master our mind.
To know thyself,
The truth to find.

In the stillness of presence,
You can be sure,
Peace on this planet,
We will procure.

PRACTICING PRESENCE

There is a presence,
In stillness, of peace within.
A blissful awareness,
Of self without sin.

The truth of our soul,
One with Source.
Cannot be strived for,
Cannot be forced.

Complete surrender,
Relax and let go.
Beneath all thoughts,
What you think you know.

Under the breath,
Within and without.
A knowing of God,
Beyond fear or doubt.

Infinite wisdom,
Perfect peace,
Absolute harmony,
Love without cease.

The only power,
The only cause.
The only effect,
Universal laws.

Spiritual beings,
Embodied on Earth,
Remembering our essence,
Our Oneness, our worth.

To change what we see,
There's nothing to do.
Practicing presence,
Makes everything new.

It touches all souls,
Awakens the heart.
Forgiveness of all,
Is where we must start.

Resting in love,
Holding the space.
Acceptance with patience,
Mercy, and grace.

Nothing to change,
To fix, or to save.
Freedom of being,
No longer a slave.

To the illusion of separation,
The cause of all pain.
There's nothing to lose,
Only to gain.

We are all One,
Connected with Source.
Practicing presence,
The greatest force.

Transforming, transmuting,
All that we see,
To a peaceful planet,
Abundant and free.

FREE AT LAST

I surrender all my sorrow,
I surrender all my pain,
I surrender all my anger,
That's keeping me insane.

I allow it to move through me,
I allow it to reveal,
All the misperceptions,
Trusting God to heal.

This is the way to Heaven,
Through the gate of Hell,
Transcending all the darkness,
At the bottom of the well.

I embrace it with compassion,
As the tears begin to flow,
Dissolving stuck emotions,
Completely letting go.

Dying to the ego's lies,
Reborn unto the soul,
Forgiving self, and others,
Remembering we are whole.

Living life in innocence,
Every moment, to unfold,
The good, Holy, and beautiful,
With a heart that's pure as gold.

No longer looking forward,
Nor looking to the past,
Living fully here and now,
I am free at last.

SACRED STILLNESS

Sacred stillness,
Beneath the breath,
A blissful aliveness,
The ego's death.

Our true essence,
Soul's divine,
Ever present,
Light we shine,

Through the darkness,
Shows the way,
Step by step,
Day by day.

From our hearts,
Deep desire,
To feel God's love,
Which we conspire.

With every breath,
Of life we breathe,
We create,
What we conceive.

Seeing clearly,
From the soul,
The highest will,
Becomes our goal.

Miracles,
Become the norm,
Manifesting,
Through our form.

Beneath the breath,
Our very source,
Sacred stillness,
The greatest force.

SINGULARITY

I've seen the singularity,
The first point of love and grace.
It appeared within the void,
Of infinite time and space.

It created an infinite plane,
Dividing the one, in two.
A second point appeared,
Another plane, cutting through.

A third point appeared,
Cutting through the two,
The Trinity, all of Creation,
Was from the One, this I knew.

From love and perfection,
Comes everything we see,
All part of the tapestry,
Of the singularity.

SOCRATES SPEAKS

The last time around,
I spoke my truth,
They made me drink the "tea,"
This time around,
So much has changed,
My right to speak is free.

My message is, much the same,
For those with ears to hear.
Question authority,
Think for yourself,
Seek truth,
Do not fear.

Those who govern,
Who bear across,
For they are only men.
Do not assume,
Their best interest is you,
As they lead you to the "lion's den."

Seek true wisdom,
Inside yourself,
The Kingdom of Heaven's within.
To know thyself,
Is the highest truth,
A revolution's about to begin.

SURRENDER THE FIGHT

Nowhere to run.
Nowhere to hide.
"Surrender the fight,"
Face the feelings inside.

Open your heart,
Don't be afraid.
See the dark images,
Of yourself, you have made.

Don't turn away,
Or judge them as wrong.
Look with compassion,
And soon they'll be gone.

The Light within,
Begins to shine bright.
Transforming and healing.
"Surrender the Fight."

Waves of emotion,
Flow through tears of pain.
Cleansing the past,
Breaking the chains.

Peace is the goal,
Keep it in sight.
There's one way to get there.
SURRENDER THE FIGHT.

SWEET AMAZING GRACE

Holy Spirit descend,
Saturate my soul,
Purify my heart,
Heal, and make me whole.

Ascend within my consciousness,
The Christ within my mind,
Such "sweet amazing grace,"
I now see, where I was blind.

I have found, what was lost,
Beneath the veil of fear,
I now believe, in only Love,
By grace, it did appear.

I am forgiven, from the past,
No future, I am free,
Wholly present, in the now,
As God created me.

Nothing to do, nowhere to go,
Like the wind, I move,
An unseen force guides me,
With nothing left to prove.

But, to teach, only Love,
The reason that I'm here,
With humility and gratitude,
A channel crystal clear.

I am the Light of the World,
The Light that never fails,
Free from chains of suffering,
The cross, and the nails.

Of myself, I do nothing,
Yet, through me, all is done,
By this "sweet amazing grace,"
The Light, the Christ, the Sun.

THE BALANCED BREATH

I am the balanced breath,
I am Spirit, in form.
In the atmosphere of polarity,
I am the "eye" of the storm.

All that spins around me,
Spins inside as well.
The electrons around a nucleus,
Of an atom, makes a cell.

The protons, and the neutrons,
A positive and negative charge.
Revolving around a central point,
A solar system, by and large.

As above, so below,
Inside, and out,
Positive and negative,
In us, is faith, and doubt.

To see one as good,
And the other one as bad,
Creates a world of duality,
Where one is happy, and one is sad.

To experience it all as neutral,
We must reside inside our core,
Where both are co-creating,
In balance, not in war.

Our bodies are our temples,
Where these "opposites" exist.
An inner state of harmony,
There's nothing to resist.

In a balanced breath,
Is the perfect yin and yang,
Where spirit and form are equal,
Created by the "big bang"

Everywhere and nowhere,
The all and the none,
From a single point of consciousness,
Our essence, we are One.

THE BLAME GAME

Humans are quite insane,
Playing the game of blame,
Believing the world outside them,
Is separate, when it's the same,

The world is a prefect mirror,
The events that are seen are YOU,
How you choose to perceive them,
And what you believe is true,

Determines your life experience,
As a victim of the world you see,
Or, as the victimizer,
Either one, you'll never be free,

Blaming the president or politics,
Religion, gender, or race,
Misperceiving the magic mirror,
That's reflecting your own face,

It's actually quite humorous,
And also quite insane,
Expecting the mirror to smile first,
All the while, you complain,

This will never change things,
In truth, we are the cause,
We are not the victims,
Of dualities limiting laws,

Until you decide to love,
Embrace and forgive the dream,
Realize who you are,
The Light, that will redeem,

We are Gods and Goddesses,
With the power to create,
We choose love and freedom,
Over separation, fear, and hate,

When we look upon the world,
With compassion, mercy, and grace,
We transcend inequities,
And have a smile upon our face,

Then the world will smile back,
Through the mirror that we see,
Ending the insane game of blame,
This truth will set us free.

THE BREATH OF LIFE

Thank you for the breath of life,
This temple I reside,
Animated by thy Light,
Darkness cannot hide.

I am the fullness of thy love,
Within my heart and mind,
Connected to thy staff and rod,
Inner peace I find.

Every breath a ceremony,
Every thought a prayer,
Every movement that I make,
Is with respect and care.

Every step that I take,
Every word I say,
Extends the Light and Love of God,
Heaven on Earth I pray.

I am an empty channel,
A clear and hollow flute,
The breath of life plays through me,
The pure and absolute.

THE ELEMENTS

Oh, Great Spirit, thank you,
For the breath of life, the air.
Thank you for our lungs,
Intaking oxygen we share.

The trees breathe in, what we breathe out,
They're the lungs of the Earth.
They breathe out, what we breathe in,
Our first inhale, at birth.

Through the water, we are born,
From the womb, of our mother.
The fountain of life, from the darkness,
Into the light, and all its color.

First, we crawl, then we walk,
Footsteps on the Earth.
Thank you for the magic soil,
We plant seeds, which give birth.

Fruits and grains, and vegetables,
That nourish every cell.
Thank you for the fire,
Transforms, and warms, as well.

Thank you for these elements,
Without which, we would die.
When we bring them into balance,
Inside ourselves, we'll fly.

Up above the surface,
Yet, grounded deep inside.
Unaffected by the illusion,
With hearts open wide.

Flying high like eagles,
With Spirit's point of view.
Rooted to the core of Earth,
Creating life anew.

Oh, Great Spirit, thank you,
For all the gifts you give.
Lead by your example,
We give back, so all may live.

We take only what we need,
We are stewards of this land.
The elements of nature,
Live or die, by our hand.

Whose hands are these, whose life is this?
Remember who we are.
Before the questions, before the problems,
The answers, not afar.

Look deep inside our heart and soul,
The stillness of the mind,
Oneness and joy for all of life,
A presence, we will find.

The Source of all Creation,
True gratefulness, and worth.
A responsibility to care,
For the elements of Earth.

For they are powerful forces,
Outside us, and inside too.
To bring them into balance,
It's up to me and you.

THE GIFT OF LIFE

My heart so full of gratitude,
For the gift of life that's free.

To touch, and taste, and feel,
To listen, speak, and see.

Free will to think, what I want,
To choose how I perceive.

The beauty of life, in everything,
All is perfect, I believe.

All made of Love, what we call God,
Connected, one, and whole.

The greatest gift, I have to share,
The wisdom of my soul.

To know the truth, to know thyself,
Is what will set us free.

The mighty I Am presence,
Lives in, as you and me.

We are it, and it is us,
In every breath we take,

Every heartbeat, every thought,
In every move we make.

We are the miracles, we are the ones,
That we've been waiting for,

To change the world,
We must change ourselves,
And tap into our core.

As powerful co-creators,
What we think, what we believe,

With gratitude, for the gift of life,
What we give, we do receive.

THE GRACE OF GOD

I accept the grace of God,
Falling, like a gentle rain.
I'm filled to overflowing,
Nothing else to attain.

Accept the realization,
That I'm worthy to receive.
I am lovable forever,
In God's eyes, I do believe.

I'm here to shine the Light,
On a world that's lost its way.
A liaison for the Lord,
To help create a brighter day.

Serving the atonement,
My purpose is revealed.
With Unconditional Love,
The sword of truth I wield.

Cutting through illusion,
Separation's veil.
The fallacy of fear,
Only Love will prevail.

The glue that binds together,
Everything we see,
The invisible magical force,
Connecting you and me.

Nothing can defy it,
No matter what they say.
No evil force can touch it,
Or make it go away.

So why not just surrender?
Accept God's grace that's free?
Believe that you are worthy,
And God's grace you will receive.

THE LIGHT OF YOUR SOUL

The Light of your Soul,
Is the God that you seek,
It can be known,
By the humble and meek.

It is not found,
In a church, or a name,
No need to exalt,
No need to blame.

Closer than breath,
Beneath all thought,
Ever present within,
No need to be sought.

The heart is a clue,
If you wish to seek,
In the stillness of Love,
Silence doth speak.

Let go of the how's,
The who's, and the why's,
Don't listen to voices,
Believe not the lies.

The truth of divinity,
Is truly divine,
All of Creation,
All space, all time.

The good and the bad,
The dark and the light,
Are one and the same,
Within God's sight.

THE MATRIX OF THE MIND

The matrix of the mind,
Dreams within dreams,
We're not actually living,
As real as it seems.

The illusion of the separate self,
Lost within a maze,
Trapped inside a house of mirrors,
Walking in a daze.

Even those that think they're spiritual,
Think they're better than the rest,
Me, me, me, my, my, my,
Surely, I'm the best.

The epitome of the ego,
Thinks it knows it all,
Only to discover,
Pride comes before the fall.

Thinking they're a healer,
A shaman, and a sage,
Wanting to be seen,
On the center of the stage,

Like a flea shouting to the Universe,
"Look at me, look at me!"
The helpless little ego,
Dying to be free.

Freedom from itself,
Yet, terrified to let go,
Its identity, attachments,
Its character in the show.

Man is not the healer,
It's a power not his own,
The lesson learned is love,
The sword and the stone.

All with good intentions,
All doing our best,
Wanting to find love,
Man's eternal quest.

Thinking it's outside us,
In circles, chasing our tails,
Not seeing nor finding,
Like trying to read braille.

Stuck behind a smokescreen,
Designed to confuse,
Wearing different masks,
So many different views.

The truth is always simple,
Hiding in plain sight,
To find it, look within,
There, you'll see the Light.

Dissolving all the shadows,
The veil that shrouds the soul,
Reveals our true identity,
Already healed and whole.

Nothing left to fix,
To change or to save,
The world of seeming duality,
No longer, we're its slave.

Trusting and allowing,
Embracing of all things,
Forgiving and transcending.
Rise up on eagle's wings.

For we have found the way,
The way of the heart,
Where all must come to enter,
The place we're all a part.

In the world , not of it,
Awake within the dream,
The matrix of the mind,
No longer is our theme.

THE PATH OF LIGHT

The path of Light,
Is not always bright.
The beauty of darkness,
Beyond physical sight.

The greatest of lessons,
Are learned when we're down.
Our biggest mistakes,
Can turn us around.

To push them away,
With judgment and blame,
Is denying the self,
Part of why it came.

Without the contrast,
Of light and dark,
Life as we know it,
Would lose its spark.

The tension between them,
Makes the world go around.
The yin and the yang,
The secret is found.

The path of Light,
Moves through it all,
Embracing life's beauty,
Whether we rise, or fall.

THE SECRET TO CHANGE

The secret to change,
The way we perceive,
We've been doing it backwards,
With what we believe.

We resist and react,
If we don't like what we see,
Thinking it will change things,
Let it be, let it be.

The secret to change,
Is a trick of the mind,
Stop chasing our tails,
One step behind.

We must use our vision,
Our inner third eye,
To see what's not here yet,
Before old ways will die.

As long as we're beating,
The drum of what is,
We'll only get more,
The same old biz.

To master our thoughts,
How and what we feel,
No matter what's happening,
What we think is real.

It's all an illusion,
Shaped by the mind,
The collective consciousness,
Of human kind.

When we awaken,
The flame of the heart,
The realization of self,
Transformation will start.

We'll realize our power,
Our free will to choose,
The world we desire,
Not the one on the news.

Don't buy into the drama,
Turn off the T.V.,
Focus on the solution,
It's within you, and me.

We are creators,
We are the cause,
We're not the effect,
Of man's limited laws.

The secret to change,
Remember who we are,
We are truly the ones,
We've been waiting for.

THE SILENT WATCHER

There is a silent watcher,
That sees only Love.
Here in the now,
Below and above.

Behind our two eyes,
In the center of our brain,
Where our Godself looks out to see,
And our ego self is slain.

Its viewpoint is always neutral,
No matter what it perceives,
With a broad inner smile,
It gives, and it receives.

A most holy presence,
The only real you.
Beyond words and thoughts,
What you say, what you do.

Humbly, patiently waiting,
For us to align,
Heart, mind, and soul,
A union, so divine.

To be guided by our source,
Is easy as 1, 2, 3.
Out of the head, into the heart,
If you want to be free.

From the prison of the self,
The walls that we build,
With all our things and stuff,
We'll never be fulfilled.

Accepting all that is,
The sacred moment of now,
Letting go, into the flow of life,
And abundance, we allow.

Everything is energy,
Made of universal mind.
That which we focus on,
We will attract, and we will find.

Things just don't happen,
"Out of the blue,"
We are co-creating,
With God, it is true.

We can create from love,
We can create from fears.
One will bring us joy,
One will bring us tears.

It's always up to us,
Which one will we choose?
How do we perceive,
What are our personal views?

How clear is our filter?
How pure is our heart?
Do we realize the Oneness?
That we are all a part?

A beautiful tapestry,
And Love's made it all.
Just open up your heart,
Rise up, and stand tall.

Be the silent watcher,
Hold the truth, of all you see,
In the highest Light and Love,
As we thinketh, so are we.

THE SOUL'S RELIGION

We are the Light emerging,
From the center of our being,
Dissolving all the veils,
Revealing what's unseen.

Beyond the forms that cast the shadows,
Is the greatest Light,
From the greatest darkness,
It shines forth, and gives us sight.

To see with eyes of judgment,
We'll never find our way,
Free from this duality,
Same shit, but different day.

If thine eye be single,
We'll see with eyes of Love,
A paradise, Heaven on Earth,
So below, as above.

The secret is perception,
It's up to us to choose,
Our thoughts, and our feelings,
We create, what we muse.

We're actually unlimited,
Infinite, and free,
We are not the victims,
Of the world we see.

For miracles to happen,
It's simply to believe,
The power of our presence,
Any wish that we conceive.

We are the genies in the bottle,
Our thoughts are commands,
With divine will, we take action,
With Love, we are God's hands.

Inspired by compassion,
Aligned with heart and mind,
Guided by our soul's religion,
Simply to be kind.

THE SOUND THAT NATURE PLAYS

Every sound that nature makes,
A symphony for the soul,
All the different living things,
Together, make a whole.

Earth, water, fire, air,
Elements to behold,
Sacred for sustaining life,
More precious than money or gold.

The Earth, Sun, Moon, and stars,
The planets and all the rest,
Galaxies, universes,
An endless treasure chest.

Here we are on this tiny speck,
Floating through infinite space,
Our purpose to remember,
The Oneness of our race.

When one is lost, we all lose,
No winners of the game,
It's time to wake up to the truth,
Our essence, we're the same.

Held within a sea of love,
The center of our heart,
The Source of all Creation,
We never can depart.

The seeming separation,
That apparently divides,
Is only an illusion,
The rise and fall of tides.

The negative and positive,
Equal opposites are the same,
The dance of duality,
Male and female that we came.

The physical reality,
A fraction that we see,
We're actually pure spirit,
Unlimited and free.

The truth that's true always,
No matter what we say,
We're all a part of everything,
The sound that nature plays.

THE SWEETNESS OF SPIRIT

As the sweetness of spirit,
Pervades every cell,
I am bathed in pure bliss,
I drink deep from this well.

An ecstatic aliveness,
So light and so fine,
Effervescent within me,
A feeling, divine.

Embraced by this Source,
I surrender, let go,
I am loved beyond measure,
By an infinite flow.

It pierces my heart,
Almost brings me to tears,
Totally vulnerable,
Without any fears.

I would rather have peace,
Than the need to be right,
No longer defending,
No desire to fight.

The war within,
Keeps the ego alive,
I raise the white flag,
My soul is revived.

As the sweetness of spirit,
Pervades every cell,
I am free, here and now,
No Heaven or Hell.

THE TAO

There is a presence,
Dynamic, yet still,
An intelligent movement,
A divine will.

Tune in, tap in,
Turn on the flow,
The life force, the prana,
That makes all things grow.

No need to pull,
Or push away,
Life and death,
Both are "the way."

The Tao, the path,
The route, the key.
Fully embracing,
Duality.

The yin and the yang,
The dark, and the light,
The tension within them,
Is not a fight.

It's the dance of life,
To live and to die,
Opposites attract,
The Earth, and the sky.

Hurricanes, tornadoes,
Floods and fire,
Nature's way,
To make us inquire.

How are we treating the Earth, our Mother?
How well are we loving our sisters and brothers?

The external imbalance,
The pollution and crime,
Effects and reflections,
Of a divided mind.

The heart knows the way,
So, seek now, inside,
Surrender to Source,
Let Love be the guide.

Unconditional and free,
Compassionate and strong,

Transcending the concept,
Of "right," and "wrong,"

An inner world of peace,
Wholeness and power,
A dynamic stillness,
Every minute, every hour.

This is the way,
The truth, and the life,
To end, the external,
Struggle, and strife.

THE TREASURE WE SEEK

When we follow our bliss,
It's impossible to miss,
The miracles and magic of life.

Every breath that we take,
Every move that we make,
Is a rhythm of harmony, not strife.

Those paths that we cross,
The gain, and the loss,
Are part of the grand design.

To raise us higher,
As we aspire,
To awaken our soul, and shine.

We are here to share,
Our gifts, so we dare,
With faith, we take a leap.

Into the unknown,
And we will be shown,
The treasure that lies in the deep.

Buried by layers of false beliefs,
That once served,
But no longer reflect.

The Light that's emerging,
The inner Source, surging,
It's nature, designed to connect.

All of the aspects,
The various facets,
Of the flawless diamond we are.

Only to discover,
We need, simply uncover,
The wound, under the scar.

To feel the pain,
Without judgment or blame,
Is the secret to peace in the heart.

To know the truth that set us free,
To know thyself,
Is where we must start.

So the treasure we seek,
Is being humble and meek,
And accepting our inheritance divine.

We are the Source,
The power and force,
It's time to let our light shine.

THE UNITY IN DUALITY

Who, and what, is right or wrong?
What is good or bad?
The belief in separation from God and self,
Is driving us quite mad!

Every single being
Has a different point of view,
Which point of view is false?
Which point of view is true?

And, of the many religions,
Which has the one true God?
The God of love, the God of fear,
Reward or punish by the rod.

Man's ideas of Heaven and Hell,
Are only states of the mind.
Divided in duality,
True peace, you'll never find.

A little war within the self,
The hidden truth to see,
To know thyself, look deep inside,
There you'll find the key.

The secret code to the gate,
Where mysteries reside,
The wisdom of the Oneness,
Where separation cannot hide.

The Love of Source holds it all,
The good, and the bad.
Judging nothing, right or wrong,
Happy, sad, or mad.

Human emotions, polarities,
Opposites, black and white,
Negative and positive attracting,
The movement, the dance of life.

One without the other,
There wouldn't be a game,
We couldn't share our differences,
We'd all be the same.

Yet, at the deepest level,
Of our being, we are One.
Celebrating our diversity,
We can really have some fun.

To end the outer struggle,
Separation, hate, and war,
To live in peace and harmony,
Can be what life is for.

Each one must find the answer,
The solution of the soul,
Apparently divided,
In our essence, we are whole.

Unwounded, safe, and powerful,
Humanly divine,
Gods and Goddesses in embryo,
Let's give birth, and shine.

Unity in duality,
As above, so below,
Heaven and Hell inside us,
The hidden truth, we now know.

Ending the little war within,
The root cause of all diss-ease,
The belief in separation,
The outer wars will cease.

TIME

Time... They say it flies,
In the moment, we arrive.

Life's events come and go,
Our attention, in the flow.

Past and future, fade away,
Memories, a different day.

Forgiving all, letting go,
Loving all, reap and sow.

Karma... Cause and effect,
Taking time to reflect.

Time to learn, time to grow,
The more we learn, the less we know.

This thing called time, can't be seen,
So, this life, what does it mean?

An illusion, trick of mind?
In silent stillness, you will find,

The time is now, there is no other,
The golden rule, love your brother.

Don't be late, be right on time,
The world is waiting, spare a dime.

Time to give, time to care,
Compassion and love, time to share.

An open heart is all it takes,
To give a hand, to heal heartbreaks.

They say time heals all wounds,
Passing time, many moons.

Everything has its place,
Infinite, eternal, time and space.

Being present, in the now,
Is the way of the Tao.

A time to laugh, a time to cry,
A time to live, a time to die.

Of the essence, it is said,
Working hard, to get ahead.

Nowhere to go, nothing to do,
Beyond time, you'll find the clue.

There's no "other" time and space,
No start or end, the human race.

Life's a circle, no beginning or end,
This thing called "time" we transcend.

At the time we arrive,
In the moment, we're alive.

TO KNOW THYSELF IS THE ANSWER

Lost in a sea of distraction,
The activity of the human mind.
The internet of illusion,
Inner peace, not easy to find.

To know thyself is the answer,
To all that we're seeking outside.
Bombarded with external stimuli,
Lost touch with our inner guide.

That which religion calls "God,"
Dwells deep within everyone's heart.
Covered by thoughts and dogma,
Preached by those we deem smart.

Man's wisdom is folly to God,
Look at the world and see.
The fruit of our labor, is rotten,
The home of the brave, is not free.

It's actually a slave corporation,
The people, the ones that are chained.
To money, and trinkets, and idols,
The media has us well trained.

The hope in a future of freedom,
Prosperity, equality, and peace,
From a political party of puppets,
The corruption will only increase.

Wars, starvation, and sickness,
Pollution, drugs, and crime.
All the result of a system,
We give energy, money, and time.

Within this sea of distraction,
Lies a shining golden key,
That opens the gates of Hweaven,
That will change everything we see.

Deep within the stillness,
In the center of our being,
The presence of God, as us resides,
The truth, of all our seeing.

To know thyself is the answer,
To every problem, one can ask.
To withdraw the mind from distraction,
And remove our ego mask.

To see the truth of who we are,
To remember what is real,
Will transform the world of suffering,
Humanity, and Earth, will heal.

TRANSFORMATION

Honesty and courage,
The surgeons of the soul.
Truth and higher wisdom,
To know thyself is the goal.

The good, the bad, the ugly,
Each treasures to behold.
The darkest of the shadows,
Brought to light, become pure gold.

Transforming and transmuting,
All that lies beneath the mask.
Hidden by denial and fear,
To feel and heal it is our task.

We can live a life of lies,
If we want to just get by.
Freedom's in transparency,
If we really want to fly.

It's time to live our truth,
Be examples to the rest.
The children are the future,
Will they be cursed, or be blessed?

It's up to us, the ones awake,
To show the way to peace.
Transform what is, from the heart,
Old ways we must release.

To tell a loving story,
No matter what's outside.
Is the secret to a different world,
Let the soul be our guide.

It knows the highest truth,
That will surely set us free.
Heaven on Earth, is here at hand,
It's up to you and me.

TRUE LOVE IS AWAKENING

True Love is awakening,
Within a distant dream,
Dissolving the duality,
Of separation's theme,

Fear, anger, suffering,
Experiences that we chose,
Through the fire, like a Phoenix,
From the ashes rose,

An ascended state of consciousness,
Centered in the core,
The Kingdom of Heaven within,
The heart's open door,

Infinite, Eternal,
Liquid love doth flow,
In us, as us, through us,
The light begins to glow,

Radiating outward,
As a lamp unto the night,
Shinning bright in darkness,
Once was blindness, now there's sight,

Illuminating from within,
Pulsating through all space,
True Love is awakening,
Within the human race...

UNITY

We gather together,
Encircle the tribe,
Anchoring in,
The "UNITY" vibe.

Lighting the grid,
It's time to thrive,
Awaken people,
We are alive!!!

Peacemakers, way showers,
Let's make a stand.
With boldness, and courage,
We take back the land!

She cannot be owned,
Bought or sold.
For money, and resources,
Oil, and gold.

We are the stewards,
She belongs not to us,
We are her children,
She's given her trust.

To nurture and protect,
With honor and care,
With love and respect,
We gather in prayer.

Claiming our freedom,
Our power to change,
The system in place,
To nature, so strange.

"UNITY" and Oneness,
Is what we decree!
Integrity and justice,
True liberty!

All created equal,
Endowed with the same,
Inalienable rights,
We stand up and claim!

No longer giving,
Our power away,
To a system of division,
With so much dismay.

We are sovereign, and free,
With power to be,
What we choose,
Who we are,
Our hearts hold the key,

That open the star gates,
To create a new Earth,
Of higher dimensions,
It's time to give birth.

Transforming,
Transmuting,
All that we see,
As we stand together,
In "UNITY."

WE ARE CO-CREATING

We are powerful co-creators,
It's time to realize.
The magic in I-magi-nation,
In what we visualize.

Centered in the heart,
Attuned to higher mind,
Grounded to the earth,
Inspiration we will find.

The purpose of our life,
Is first to be aligned.
Attaining peace within ourselves,
And sharing with mankind.

From this inner Source,
Of love and harmony,
We'll sing our song with joy,
For everyone to see.

Healing all the suffering,
Poverty, and war,
Nurturing the children's souls,
Our future, we will soar.

We are powerful co-creators,
With God's all-pervading force.
If we don't like where we're headed,
We can change the course.

First, we must conceive,
A higher truth and believe.
Mastering our thoughts,
And our actions, to achieve.

Anything we dream of,
Our wishes are commands.
The universe will orchestrate,
Trust it's in God's hands.

With free will as our greatest gift,
To think, and choose, and be.
Anything our hearts desire,
Our souls are truly free.

WE THE PEOPLE

We the people, are awakening,
From the shadows in "the cave,"
Seeing through the matrix,
From which we've been enslaved.

As mist rises from a lake,
Reflections become clear,
Of all the things around us,
That we've been taught to fear.

Looking deep within ourselves,
The truth of who we are,
Seeing God in everything,
On Earth, and distant stars.

Heaven on Earth is ours to be,
As above, and so below,
Breaking chains that bound us,
The weight we used to tow.

Remembering our freedom,
To think, and choose, and be.
Creating anything we wish,
Imagination is the key.

Unlocks our higher purpose,
For which we all have come.
Marching to a different beat,
Our heart, a different drum.

It's Love that is the answer,
To all the world's misdeeds.
Compassion through our action,
Solving everybody's needs.

It's time to come out, from "the cave,"
And stand within the light.
Stretch our wings, jump for joy,
Reclaiming our birthright.

Flying high like eagles,
Nesting in a tree.
Our vision of the world is new,
We the people,
Are awakened,
And free.

WHAT IS LOVE

What is Love?
They say, it hurts,
True Love heals,
Fake love flirts.

One feels light,
The other feels dark,
One's a flame,
The other, a spark.

One gives life,
The other one takes,
One builds up,
The other one breaks.

One for-"gives,"
The other for-"gets,"
One gives joy,
The other, regrets.

One sustains,
The other one dies,
One is true,
The other one lies.

One is patient,
And oh, so kind,
It sees clearly,
The other one's blind.

One is humble,
And not so proud,
One is quiet,
The other one, loud.

One always hopes,
And perseveres,
The other one, jealous,
And full of fears.

One is trusting,
And protects,
The other one judges,
And projects.

One holds honor,
And respects,
The other disgraces,
And rejects.

One never fails,
And never hurts,
The other betrays,
And deserts.

Yet, both are held,
By Love's embrace,
With endless compassion,
Mercy, and grace.

Love is free,
And can't be bought,
Unconditional Love
Gives all it's got.

Without expecting,
Anything back,
An infinite Source,
It knows not lack.

Love is the answer,
Love is the cure,
The only purpose,
Of what life is for.

WHO ARE WE

Some say we're simply monkeys,
Some say we're souls divine.
Some say we're gods in embryo,
Let's start with "human kind..."

Compassion towards all life,
Kindness to one another,
Love your neighbor as yourself,
And loving our Earth Mother.

The world seems so divided,
Different colors, different tribes.
We're actually interdependent,
A symphony of various vibes.

Will we play in harmony?
The music that makes life.
Will we keep on bickering?
Creating stress and strife.

Who are we, here and now,
Forgiving all that's past.
The answer to the question,
That everyone must ask.

To find the truth, to know thyself,
Is why we all are here.
We're both human and divine,
It's becoming crystal clear.

Perfectly imperfect,
No better, or no worse.
The idea of original sin,
Has been our only curse.

It was actually original blessing,
That happened at "the fall."
If it wasn't for duality,
We wouldn't be here at all.

Life is how you look at it,
We are free to choose.
The fun is in playing the game,
Not whether you win or lose.

The last will be first,
The first will be last.
The blueprint of nature is balance,
No matter how slow or fast.

Patience is a virtue,
Kindness is the key,
To be human and divine,
Is what will set free.

HEARTS AND MINDS ALIGNED

Where two or more are gathered,
It's written, "I am there,"
An invisible powerful presence,
We commune in prayer.

The purest prayer is gratitude,
Love always perseveres,
Surrendering the ego's will,
With its judgments and fears.

We join with hearts wide open,
Channels for the divine,
Sharing the fruits of spirit,
As branches of the vine.

As we give, we receive,
And reap what we sow,
From the goodness of our souls,
We each help love to grow.

This is our only purpose,
With compassion, mercy, and grace,
Transforming the world of suffering,
Healing the whole human race.

A simple choice to be made,
Conditions do not define,
Our power to re-create,
With hearts and minds aligned.

To perceive the perfection in everything,
Is the secret to permanent change,
To try to change the outside first,
To the nature of Spirit is strange.

Spirit sees and knows the truth,
That only Love is real,
Whatever the appearances,
They never can conceal.

The truth that's true always,
From Oneness we have come,
There is no separation,
One heart, one beat, one drum.

Where two or more are gathered,
Our energy combined,
Nothing is impossible,
With hearts and minds aligned.

In the silence, in the stillness, the voice of God you'll hear, whispering words of wisdom. There is nothing to fear. The truth that's true always: that we and God are One. "We are the Light of the World." We are all born of Love, and that is the only thing that is real. Our treasure is in Heaven; no thief could ever steal. Heaven is here among us if we have eyes to see. The eye of the needle that every soul must pass through; to face our fears unaffected, by knowing what is true. We are infinite, eternal. We are pure Spirit, the Light of the World, One with God. We are whole.

—*Socrates The Messenger*

Socrates The Messenger

Socrates is a poet, philosopher, and healer. Born in Washington, D.C., he became a competitive bodybuilder, which led him to appearing on various talk shows. He was inspired to move to Los Angeles, CA to become a model and actor, and ended up on the set of *Baywatch*. While doing a juice fast to prepare for an interview with Chippendales, he had a Spiritual awakening.

An "inner voice" guided him to study the healing arts and become a massage therapist and Reiki practitioner.

He moved to Sedona, AZ, and the inner voice started speaking in Rhymes. He was inspired to take pen to paper.

In the early 2000s, Socrates was guided to the Appalachian Mountains by Higher Beings. Gracefully, in 2021 he was able to leave the Earth Plane at the magical Healing Waters Wilderness, his home in the forest where he was guided to, where he practiced the healing arts alongside the love of his life, Angela.